The HISTORY of our BIBLE

by P. J. HUNT

with illustrations by ERIC WINTER

Ladybird Books Ltd Loughborough

Caedmon

About 1300 years ago, a man named Caedmon worked as a cowherd in the grounds of Whitby Abbey in Yorkshire. The Abbey was ruled by the Abbess Hilda, who had been a royal princess.

Some of the monks in the Abbey worked on beautifully lettered and decorated manuscripts (known as 'illuminated' manuscripts) which were in Latin, and which few ordinary people could understand. Others worked on the farm or in the fields or about the building itself. At evening-time, they all gathered together in the big hall for their meal.

After supper, it was the custom for those at the table to take turns singing songs and glees to the accompaniment of a harp. The harp was passed round from man to man, and each was expected to sing when the harp came to him.

Caedmon could not sing, and the sight of the harp coming nearer and nearer to him made him very depressed and miserable.

One night, as the harp came very close, Caedmon rose from the table and went out into the darkness to his cowshed. There, tired with the day's work, he fell asleep and had a dream.

Caedmon leaves the table as the harp comes nearer

0 7214 0289 5

Caedmon's dream

He dreamed that the whole stable was lit by a strong, bright light, and that when he looked up, he saw an angel, who said—

"Caedmon, sing some songs to me."

Caedmon answered that he could not sing, but the angel persisted and so he tried. In his dream he was amazed to realize that he could sing. When he awoke he sang a song and found that his voice was better than he had thought.

The Abbess was so impressed when Caedmon told her of his dream that she ordered Caedmon to be taken into the Abbey as a Brother to compose songs.

He sang songs about the Creation, about the Children of Israel, about Jesus and the Early Church, all in language that ordinary people understood. Visitors to the Abbey learnt the songs and went away singing, so that others heard and learnt them too; and soon people could be heard singing Caedmon's songs as they worked.

Caedmon had made the Bible come alive. For the first time many people heard the stories we read about in the Bible. No longer was God's Word known only to those who knew Latin.

Caedmon dreams that an angel asks him to sing

The work of Bede

A few years before Caedmon's death, a man called Bede was born in 673 A.D. near Monkwearmouth in Durham. While he was yet a boy, his parents died, and Bede was sent to the monastery of Wearmouth. He grew up to be a great scholar and lived his life in and around Jarrow.

Bede devoted his life to the study of the Scriptures and to teaching and writing. Both the monasteries with which he was connected—Jarrow and Monkwearmouth—had splendid libraries containing many hand-written books and manuscripts. From them Bede learnt all he could about science, astronomy, the Greek language and many other subjects.

Bede's writings tell us a great deal of what we know today of life in early Britain. He wrote a book called 'The Ecclesiastical History of England' and also many commentaries on various parts of the Bible.

He loved his work of translating parts of the Bible into the common language, for he wished everyone to have at least the Lord's Prayer and the Apostle's Creed firmly in their minds in a language which they could understand. He gave priests copies of these to help them to inspire the people under their care.

Bede working in the monastery library

Bede's last hours

Bede was still working on his translation of St. John's Gospel as his life drew near its end. He was most anxious to finish it before he died.

It was the evening before Ascension Day, 735 A.D., and his strength was failing rapidly ; but Bede, on his sick-bed, was determined to finish the work. By his side sat his scribe, carefully writing to Bede's dictation.

"How much more is there?" asked Bede.

"Only one chapter," answered the scribe. "Will it be too much for you, master?"

"No, no," said the old man. "Take thy pen and write quickly."

So the work continued until the last sentence was finished and the scribe was able to say, "It is completed now, master. The whole of St. John's Gospel in our own tongue!"

"Lift me and carry me to the window," said Bede.

The scribe did so, and Bede, chanting the Gloria— 'Glory be to the Father, and to the Son, and to the Holy Ghost,' died peacefully and happily.

The dying Bede dictates to a scribe

The young Alfred

Over a century after Bede's death, Ethelwulf, King of Wessex, brought a new Queen, called Judith, to England. Ethelwulf had five sons, and one day Judith discovered that none of them could read. She showed them a beautiful book of Saxon poetry, saying that whichever son should learn to read first should have the book for his own.

The youngest, Alfred, was very keen to win, and he worked so hard that he won the book. We should remember that it was not easy to learn to read in those days, because there were so few books and so few people who could read or write.

Alfred became very keen on learning; when he was only thirteen he was able to translate some of the psalms and prayers from Latin into Anglo-Saxon, the common language of the day.

In 871 A.D., at the age of twenty-two, he became King of Wessex. At this period the Danes were constantly making ferocious attacks on the coasts—and during those battles, Alfred's brothers had been killed. Although Alfred had many battles with the Danes, he was also able to make a peace treaty with them.

 Queen Judith shows a book to Ethelwulf's five sons

Alfred—a true Christian king

Alfred drew up a law-book in order to give his people good government, and at the beginning of this book he wrote down the Ten Commandments, saying that "they are God's law and better than man's."

He invited to his court learned men from all parts of Europe, men whose knowledge would help him in his great plan of educating the people of England. Alfred realised that religion and learning were two most important parts of life, and he wished the clergy to be educated well enough to teach their people properly.

Alfred, the royal scholar, was in his own life a truly Christian king, and it was his wish that all the freeborn youth in his kingdom should be able to read the Scriptures well. He knew that God's law was the most important law by which men should live.

He lived for the good of his people and put aside all personal aims and ambitions in order to devote himself wholly to the welfare of the people whom he ruled.

In addition to ruling, he worked hard at translating famous Latin manuscripts into Anglo-Saxon.

King Alfred invites to his Court learned men from other countries

John Wycliffe

John Wycliffe was a Yorkshireman, born about the year 1320. He was a learned man and held an important post as principal of Balliol College, Oxford.

He felt that a great deal was wrong with the Church at that time, and that someone must start putting it right.

"If the Church were not so rich," he said, "it might be better able to do its work and thus serve people properly. It should become more humble and more like Christ."

He was distressed that the clergy were not interpreting the Word of God correctly, and he taught that people should only believe those clergy whose own lives were good examples of Christian living. He knew, too, that the Bible was the only real authority on many difficult questions.

Later Wycliffe became vicar of Lutterworth in Leicestershire, and felt he must teach more about God's laws; for he realized that people could not live Christian lives if they did not know these laws. So he trained a band of men and sent them out into the countryside to teach the people. Soon there was such a large number of these followers that many people began to hear of Wycliffe's views.

Wycliffe sends his followers to teach the people

Wycliffe translates the Bible

Wycliffe soon realized that it was of little use to teach people how to live good lives if they knew nothing about God, Who is the source of that life. In other words, he felt that God's Word should be translated from Latin into a language which they could understand. He therefore decided that he must translate the Latin Bible into English. In this he was helped by his friend Nicholas de Hereford.

Can you imagine what a huge task that translation must have been? Look at one page in your Bible and think how long it would take merely to copy out that page by hand in your own language—let alone translate it into another language! If you look at the number of pages in the Bible, you will realize what an enormous work Wycliffe undertook.

However his teachings were not popular, and in 1382 he was brought to London, tried and declared a heretic—a word used to describe any person whose belief was thought to be contrary to the faith or dogma of the Church. His works were condemned to be burnt and his followers imprisoned. He was allowed to retire to Lutterworth and, though ill, he continued his translation work helped by his curate, John Purvey.

At last the work was finished, and for the first time, there was a Bible in the English language.

Wycliffe at work on his translation

Hearing the Bible in everyday language

The one Bible at Lutterworth was of little use on its own. It had to be copied and re-copied, so that there could be enough copies to send throughout the country.

The men whom Wycliffe had appointed took them out, and since there were not many people who could read, it became the custom to gather in church or round the market crosses or on the village greens, to hear one of Wycliffe's men read the Bible aloud. These men were known as 'poor preachers', 'poor priests' or 'Lollards'. They were dressed in rough clothes and preached in simple words which people could understand.

It must have been wonderful to hear the Bible for the very first time in one's own language. Some people wanted to take the Book home so that they could try and read it themselves; others asked to buy it. One farmer offered the preacher a load of hay in exchange for permission to borrow the Book for a short time each day. But the preachers could not part with their copies, for they were needed to take to the next village to be read to the people there.

Because of his reforming zeal, Wycliffe has been called the 'Morning Star of the Reformation'.

One of Wycliffe's followers reads to the people

Printing

Copying by hand was a slow, laborious business and could never meet the ever-growing demand for Bibles.

About the year 1450, a man called Johann Gutenberg, who lived in Mainz in Germany, began to experiment with moveable type for printing. He made wooden letters from the bark of trees and dipped them in dye, and found that, when pressed on to parchment, the shape of the letters could be reproduced. By putting the letters side by side, he found he could make copies of words and even whole pages. Instead of having one copy of a book, it was now possible to have hundreds. In this way, he produced the first printed book in Europe—a Latin Bible. Education was spreading, and Latin was the language used by educated people.

In England, William Caxton set up a printing press; and the influence of printing and books spread among the people.

The desire to read and obtain more knowledge increased rapidly and colleges and schools were built in Oxford, Cambridge and other places.

At work on a printing press in the time of Gutenberg

William Tyndale

After John Wycliffe's death, the poor preachers were stopped from selling the Bible, and anyone who translated any part was threatened with imprisonment or death. The leaders of Church and State felt it was too dangerous a book for ordinary people to read.

But Wycliffe's Bible was still copied in secret by men who awaited another leader who would fearlessly defy such laws.

About 1490, William Tyndale was born. He was well-educated at Oxford and at Cambridge, and was much inspired by the clever Dutch scholar, Erasmus. Tyndale was prepared to defy the law in order to carry on Wycliffe's work.

One day, he happened to declare in company that he wished *all* men could read the Bible in English. When his hearers pointed out to him that to translate the Bible was forbidden by Parliament and the Pope, Tyndale burst out angrily, "I defy the Pope and all his laws. If God spares my life, e'er many years I will make the boy who drives the plough to know more of the Bible than do many priests!"

The people listening were very shocked, and after that Tyndale became a marked man.

Tyndale makes his defiant speech to a group of shocked listeners

Tyndale's work of translation

After this speech, Tyndale went to London to work on the big task he had set himself, that of translating Erasmus's Greek Testament into English.

There he approached the Bishop of London, Bishop Tunstall, to try and interest him in the translation; but the Bishop would have nothing to do with it and said he had no room in his palace for the carrying on of such work.

Tyndale tried elsewhere and found a friend in a wealthy cloth-merchant named Humphrey Monmouth, who offered him a home, money and protection for his work. There he carried on in secret, well aware that he had many enemies. He knew there was always the danger of arrest, for the bishops were much against a Bible which ordinary people could read.

As Tyndale worked, his pile of translated sheets grew, and he began to fear for their safety. If the house were raided Monmouth might well be imprisoned for giving him shelter, and the sheets might be seized and destroyed. He wrote later, "I perceived that not only in my Lord of London's palace, but in all England, there was no room for attempting a translation of the Scriptures."

Tyndale at work in Monmouth's house

Tyndale flees the country

So Tyndale decided it was not safe for him to stay in England any longer. He was not fearful for his own life, but he knew that if he were caught his work would be stopped. He could not bear the thought that this might happen before his task was finished.

One night he slipped out of Monmouth's house and, looking round anxiously in case he was being followed, he made his way warily down to London's wharves. He had his precious manuscript and the pages which he had already translated hidden away in his baggage, and he succeeded in reaching the wharf in safety, where he boarded a sailing ship bound for Antwerp. He never set foot in his own land again.

From Antwerp he went to Hamburg, and there found friends who were willing to help and even to risk death in order that the English people might read the Bible in their own language.

The work was still extremely dangerous, for spies seemed to be everywhere, and Tyndale lived in constant fear that his work might be seized and destroyed. Observing the utmost secrecy, he worked harder than ever to complete his English New Testament.

Tyndale escapes at night

Tyndale finds a printer

At last Tyndale's English New Testament was finished. Now he faced a new problem. He had to find someone courageous enough to print copies for him. There was no-one in Hamburg willing to help, but after much secret enquiry Tyndale heard of a printer in Cologne whose name was Peter Quentel and who was in sympathy with the cause. Quentel also had friends among the English merchants in Cologne.

Tyndale's enemies were as active as ever, and it was necessary to take the greatest care that the printing plans were not discovered. Each night Tyndale made his way through the darkness to the printing works. There he checked the first copy of every printed page to make sure there were no errors before further copies were made.

When he was satisfied that the proof was accurate, the printing presses went into action so that hundreds of copies could be made for despatch to England.

The printing of this translation began in the year 1525. Not only Tyndale himself, but Quentel and his apprentices had to be most careful that no-one discovered the secret work they were doing.

Tyndale discusses a proof sheet of his English New Testament with the printer

Tyndale betrayed

Suddenly one night, a messenger arrived with the dreadful news that Tyndale had been betrayed! Already the servants of the Pope were on the way to seize the precious manuscript and the type. There was not a moment to lose!

Feverishly Tyndale gathered together his manuscripts and printed sheets and rushed out of the house—just in time. His enemies arrived almost immediately afterwards, and though they made a frantic search they could find no trace of the English Bible.

The man who had betrayed Tyndale was John Cochlaeus. Having failed to capture Tyndale in Cologne, he then warned King Henry VIII of England to have all the English ports watched.

But Tyndale was not on his way to England at all. He was sailing up the Rhine to the city of Worms, where he had friends and where he knew he could find refuge.

Six months later, the work was finished, and Tyndale held in his hands the first complete copy of his New Testament printed in English.

His vow, that he would give the English ploughboy a chance of knowing the Scriptures, was now nearer fulfilment.

Tyndale hurriedly collects his manuscripts to save them from his enemies

Tyndale's work is burnt

It was not long before hundreds of copies of the printed New Testament had been made and sent to Antwerp. From there merchants smuggled the copies into England. They packed them in amongst other goods to make them look like ordinary merchandise, for they knew that all the ports were being watched.

The enemies examined all goods landing in England, and whenever they discovered any Bibles, they burned them on the quayside. However, some got through, and brave people were able to pass them on to others.

Tyndale then had the Bible printed in smaller type so that the book itself would be smaller and easier to smuggle. Copies were sent to quiet, out-of-the-way ports, sometimes in fishing boats, sometimes hidden in sacks of flour or at the bottom of barrels filled with other things. In this way, large numbers of Bibles came into England under the very noses of Tyndale's enemies.

The Bishop of London then tried other plans to get rid of the Book. He offered large sums of money for every copy found. A friend of Tyndale's heard of this and sold him many copies so that he could give Tyndale the money with which to print more Bibles. So instead of hindering Tyndale's work, the bishop was actually helping it!

 Burning smuggled copies of Tyndale's New Testament

Miles Coverdale

One day, however, Tyndale was again betrayed by a spy who pretended to be an admirer of his beliefs and work, with the result that Tyndale was imprisoned and condemned to death. His last words were, 'Lord, open the King of England's eyes,' a prayer which was answered, before many years had passed.

The work had to go on, and the man who continued it was Miles Coverdale, who completed a new version, dedicated to the King, in 1535.

The demand for the Bible in English was now growing, and Henry VIII, on Archbishop Cranmer's advice, felt it wise to allow Coverdale's Bible to be published in England.

Another version, in 1537, known as 'Matthew's Bible', was also authorised by Henry VIII; in 1539 Coverdale produced a revised Bible, called the Great Bible because of its size.

On September 5th 1538, a royal proclamation stated that a Bible must be placed in every church in the land. So popular were these Bibles that they often had to be chained to the reading-desks so that people could not take them away. Many people who could not read clamoured round anyone who could, asking that the Bible be read aloud to them.

Reading the Bible to the people

The Geneva Bible and the Authorised version

During the reign of Mary Tudor, who was a Roman Catholic, the Protestants were again persecuted and Archbishop Cranmer was amongst those who were burnt at the stake. An order was made that all the Bibles must be taken out of the churches, and anyone found possessing the Book was sent to the dungeons.

In Geneva, the reformer John Calvin started a Protestant state, and was joined by Miles Coverdale and, amongst others, an Englishman named William Whittingham. They decided that what was needed, instead of more cumbersome 'Great' Bibles, was a smaller, cheaper edition which men could carry around in their pockets. In 1560 their version, known as the Geneva Bible, was published and a copy was presented to Queen Elizabeth I on her accession. It was the first Bible in which the chapters were divided into separate verses.

When James I came to the throne, he thought there were too many translations of the Bible available, and that there should be one good translation which would replace all others. So, in 1611, the 'Authorised Version' was produced under James' authority, and this became a most popular version and was used for more than three centuries.

 Presenting a copy of the Geneva Bible to Queen Elizabeth I

A find in a waste-paper basket

In 1844 there lived a German scholar called Tischendorf, who was interested in the study of ancient manuscripts.

One day he visited a lonely monastery on Mount Sinai, and as he wandered around he noticed a large waste-paper basket full of what seemed to be old paper.

"What's that?" he asked.

"Only old rubbish," replied the monk in charge. "We have already burnt most of it."

Trying not to show his excitement, Tischendorf asked if he might look through it and was given permission. He had not searched very far before he was amazed to find some leaves of the oldest Bible he had ever seen—a manuscript transcribed probably not later than the 4th century. The Abbot said he might buy some, and Tischendorf took as many leaves as he could afford. He presented these to King Frederick-Augustus II of Saxony, and they became known as the Codex Frederico-Augustanus in his honour.

Tischendorf was not a rich man, and it was not until nine years later that he had saved up enough money to travel east again. He was anxious to find out whether all the other leaves about which the monk had spoken had really been burnt.

Tischendorf finds some leaves of an ancient Bible

Tischendorf's further discoveries

In 1853, Tischendorf went to the monastery on Mount Sinai again. This time the monks were not so helpful and all that they would let him take away was a fragment containing a few verses of Genesis.

In 1859, he went back for a third time. On this visit he decided it might be wiser not to mention his interest in manuscripts too soon. On his last night there, the monastery steward said, "I too have an old manuscript," and from a high shelf above the door, he took down a bulky parcel. He unwrapped it and Tischendorf was thrilled to see the pages he had seen in the basket fifteen years before and had been unable to buy!

Not wishing to keep such a treasure to himself, he asked if he might borrow the volume overnight to copy some of it. He was given this permission. Next morning, he persuaded the Abbot to send it to another monastery in Cairo, where Tischendorf was able to go and continue working on it.

Eventually the monks there sent it to the Tsar of Russia and, years later, it was bought by the British Government and placed in the British Museum. It is called Codex Sinaiticus.

 A monk hands more manuscripts to Tischendorf

Mary Jones

In a poor cottage in Wales around 1800 lived 10-year-old Mary Jones. She could not read, but her father used to tell her Bible stories, although the Jones family did not possess a Bible. Nearby there lived a rich farmer named Evans. He had a Bible, and his wife said that if ever Mary learnt to read she might go to their house and read it.

When a school opened two miles away, Mary gladly walked there each day in order to learn to read. Soon she became a good reader. However, she still wanted her own Bible, and so began to save every penny she could earn. It took her six years to save enough to buy one.

Then she heard that a Mr. Charles at Bala, 25 miles away, had some Welsh Bibles to sell; the only way to get there was to walk, and so one morning she set off, barefoot, carrying her only pair of shoes so that she might save them to wear when she reached Bala. But Mr. Charles had only three Bibles left, and these he had already promised to other people. When he saw Mary's disappointment he was troubled and decided to let her have one, saying that perhaps someone else would wait a little longer. Mary was delighted and hurried back over the hills with her precious Bible. Soon she was reading its stories to her mother and father.

Some time afterwards Mr. Charles visited London and told a group of people about Mary. They decided to start a society which would supply people all over the world with Bibles in their own language. That society exists today and is the British & Foreign Bible Society.

Mary Jones sets out on her 25-mile walk

The Dead Sea Scrolls

On the shores of the Dead Sea, not far from Jericho, lies the barren region of Qumran. One day, in 1947, two shepherd boys were searching for a straying animal in this wild desert when one of them noticed a gap in the rocks. Idly, he threw a stone in and, to his surprise, he heard a noise of breaking.

He and his friend crawled through the hole to find out what had been hit, and found themselves in a large cave. Around them were numbers of tall jars containing what seemed to be rolls of decaying leather. The boys did not know what they were but they took some away and tried to sell them.

At first no-one seemed interested, until a clever professor discovered that one roll was an early version of the Book of Isaiah.

Excited scholars returned to Qumran and found more caves containing more scrolls. All the scrolls had to be treated extremely carefully, especially when they were being unrolled, so that they were not damaged; with the help of scientists some hundreds of pieces of the Bible—all very ancient—were found and preserved. It is thought they were hidden there to save them from destruction by enemies of the writers of the scrolls.

The finding of the Dead Sea Scrolls

Modern versions and translations

Today, although the Bible is a 'best-seller', there are still many people who have not yet heard a word of the Gospel. Millions of Bibles are sent all over the world, often distributed by travelling salesmen, called 'colporteurs', who go on foot or bicycle or sometimes in a van, taking the Scriptures to places which are often difficult to reach.

Translations are still being made, for language is ever-changing, making revisions necessary every so often. Bible translation is especially difficult because many languages do not have just the right words to express some religious truths

In Britain, too, we have various modern translations, in addition to the Authorised Version. For instance, there is the Revised Version, the translations of Dr. James Moffatt and of Canon J. B. Phillips, the Jerusalem Bible, the New English Bible and several others.

The Bible is not one book; it is sixty-six different books: the thirty-nine books of the Old Testament tell about God and the world before Jesus came to earth; and the twenty-seven books of the New Testament tell of Jesus's life on earth, and about the Early Church afterwards.

A colporteur sets out in his van

Distributing the Bible today

Today at Bible House, the headquarters of the British & Foreign Bible Society in London, the work goes on. A trained team of manuscript examiners checks each version of the Bible as it is made. This alone costs £70,000 per year.

Every year the printing and binding experts produce over five million volumes in England for the Society, as well as the large numbers which are produced overseas. The United Bible Societies, a thirty-five member strong 'fellowship of Bible Societies', of which the British & Foreign Bible Society is a leading member, between them distribute on average over 100 million copies of Scriptures each year; they have translated the Scriptures into more than 1,326 different languages.

Each working day over six tons of the Scriptures are despatched from Bible House. They are packed into big wooden boxes, labelled and shipped to countries overseas.

The history of our Bible shows us the priceless heritage we have. When our present Queen was crowned, a copy of the Bible was handed to her with the words "We present you with this book—the most valuable thing this world affords. Here is Wisdom—this is the Royal Law—these are the lively oracles of God."

Despatching Bibles to overseas countries

Series 649
A Ladybird Book